A Basic Guide to

SOCCER

An Official U.S. Olympic Committee Sports Series

The U.S. Olympic Committee

Griffin Publishing

First printing 1995

10 9 8 7 6 5 4 3 2 1

ISBN 1-88180-35-6

Griffin Publishing

544 Colorado Street
Glendale, California 91204
Telephone: 1-818-244-2128 / Fax 1-818-242-1172

Manufactured in the United States of America

Acknowledgments

PUBLISHER

Robert M. Howland
President, Griffin Publishing

USOC

United States Olympic Committee
John Krimsky, Jr, *Executive Director*
One Olympic Plaza
Colorado Springs, CO 80909-5760

SERIES EDITOR

Richard D. Burns, Ph.D.

SENIOR EDITOR/WRITER

Joey Lorraine Parker

PRODUCTION EDITOR

Larry Davis

BOOK DESIGN

Mark M. Dodge

PHOTO EDITOR

Robin L. Howland

CONSULTING EDITOR

Bob Mathias

CONTRIBUTING EDITORS

American Youth Soccer Organization

US Soccer Federation

Paul Harris

PHOTO CREDITS

Allsport Photography

Sandra B. Applegate

Phil Stephens Photography

World Cup /Lynne Meterparel

Griffin Publishing wishes to thank the American Medical Association, the American Dental Association, Edward L. Garr, M.D. and Ray Padilla, D.D.S. for their contributions.

Editorial Statement

In the interest of brevity, the Editors have chosen to use the standard English form of address. Please be advised that this usage is not meant to suggest a restriction to, nor an endorsement of, any individual or group of individuals, either by age, gender, or athletic ability. The Editors certainly acknowledge that boys and girls, men and women, of every age and physical condition are actively involved in sports and we encourage everyone to enjoy the sports of his or her choice.

On behalf of the United States Olympic Committee,

Welcome to the Olympic Sports Series

We are extremely pleased to inaugurate the Olympic Sports Series. This unique series will encourage parents, athletes of all ages and novices who are thinking about a sport for the first time, to get involved with the challenging and rewarding world of Olympic sports.

This series of paperback books covers both summer and winter sports, features Olympic history and basic sports fundamentals, and encourages family involvement. Each book includes information on how to get started in a particular sport, including equipment and clothing; rules of the game; health and fitness; basic first aid; and guidelines for spectators. Of special interest is the information on opportunities for senior citizens, volunteers and physically challenged athletes. In addition, each book is enhanced by photographs and illustrations and a complete, easy-to-understand glossary.

Because this family-oriented series neither assumes nor requires prior knowledge of a particular sport it can be enjoyed by all age groups. Regardless of anyone's level of sports knowledge, playing experience or athletic ability, this official U.S. Olympic Committee Sports Series will encourage understanding and participation in sports and fitness.

The purchase of these books will assist the 1996 U.S. Olympic Team. This series supports the Olympic mission and serves importantly to enhance participation in the Olympic and Pan American Games.

John Krimsky, Jr.
Executive Director

Contents

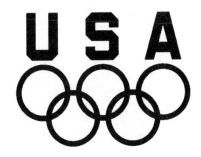

Olympic Creed

The most important thing in the Olympic Games is not to win but to take part, just as the most important thing in life is not the triumph but the struggle. The essential thing is not to have conquered but to have fought well.

These famous words, commonly referred to as the Olympic Creed, were spoken by Baron Pierre de Coubertin, founder of the modern Olympic Games, following the Congress of Paris in 1894. They aptly describe the theme behind each and every Olympic competition.

SOCCER AND THE OLYMPICS

Although soccer did not appear in the Olympics until the Paris Games of 1900, it is actually one of the world's oldest sports. A brief summary of the historical origins and early development of the game is in order here.

The Origins of Soccer

Historical evidence suggests that soccer was played in both Babylon and early Egypt and was especially popular throughout the Greek and Roman Empires.

The early Greeks called the game "harpaston" and the rules were very similar to modern Rugby. Harpaston was more than a game; it was a primary means of conditioning Spartan warriors. Running increased a man's stamina, and ball control movements improved his timing and coordination—both of which were just as important to ancient warriors as they are to today's athletes. So important was this conditioning that the soldiers were ordered to play a game of harpaston every day, no matter where they were! As a result, Roman soldiers took the game with them into foreign countries and even taught the native people how to play.

With the decline of the Roman Empire and the onset of the troubled Dark Ages, harpaston all but disappeared. Fortunately, soccer was too popular to be forgotten entirely, and during the Renaissance a new form of soccer called "calcio" was introduced in Italy. This game was very similar to harpaston and was widely played in both Italy and England throughout the Middle Ages.

In England, soccer's popularity grew to the extent that by the early 1300s, during the reign of King Edward II, palace military advisors began to view the game as a riotous nuisance and a serious threat to national security. To understand why they felt this way, we have to take a brief look at the changes in military strategy.

During the Roman Empire, invading armies made numerous attempts to conquer Rome, Constantinople, Alexandria, and other major centers. To protect the Empire's capital cities, Roman warriors marched long distances to intercept the invaders and turn them back. Marching required stamina, and playing soccer was an excellent means of improving and strengthening the soldiers' legs and overall physical condition. By the 1300s, however, British military strategy was markedly different from that of its Roman predecessor; primarily in that it assumed offensive, rather than defensive, tactics. English soldiers were more apt to be stationed behind castle walls than to traverse the countryside, and from there they were expected to defend their nation by the use of bows and arrows. As the successful application of the bow and arrow requires skill, and skill requires practice, it is understandable why England's military advisors were outraged when they discovered that soldiers were spending their leisure time not in practicing archery, but in playing soccer!

In England, especially, it was not uncommon for more than 500 players to participate in each game, and soccer was becoming so rough that injuries were extensive. Moreover, since there were no designated playing fields (nor any boundary rules), games were played on public streets, sometimes stretching the length of an entire town! In the absence of rules, anything could be done to move the ball. So riotous were these competitions that after every game, shopkeepers had to replace their storefront windows, and farmers complained that cows and goats were too upset to give milk. Something had to be done— "soccermania" was getting out of hand.

In 1314, King Edward II issued a proclamation forbidding the game in England and ordered the people to get back to work. Anyone caught playing soccer when he should be working would be punished. Once again, soccer went into a period of decline, but it never completely disappeared.

During the reign of Queen Elizabeth I, England had become the dominant economic and military force in Western Europe, and the people were anxious to celebrate. Prosperity afforded the working class a modest amount of leisure time; and since the invention of firearms rendered archery practice unnecessary, the people looked for a way to amuse themselves. By 1603, on the day of the coronation of King James I, soccer (or football as it was now called), was once again publicly acknowledged—and King James actually encouraged his subjects to play! Soccer was off and running, and has never looked back.

Fortunately, civilization extended its influence onto the playing field and the new games were never as rough as were their predecessors. The ideas of sportsmanship and fair play were starting to take root—concepts which never would have troubled soccer's primitive ancestors!

By the early nineteenth century, soccer clubs were being formed all over Europe. Rules had not yet been determined so each club simply made up their own—an approach which caused hotly contested matches. Finally, in 1862 at Cambridge, England, an attempt was made to generate a uniform code of rules. Mr. J. C. Thing published his *Ten Rules* for what he called "The Simplest Game." One year later (and with a few modifications), the Cambridge University Football Rules were established.

Soccer in the Olympics

Throughout the 1800s, soccer's popularity spread throughout Europe. Not only were the English and the Italians diehard soccer enthusiasts, the Scandinavians took to the sport with equal gusto. With such wide-range geographic interest, organizers of the 1900 Olympic Games in Paris, France, voted to include soccer as a full-medal sport. They were not disappointed. Attendance was standing-room-only for each match, and the games were exciting for fans and players alike.

With its new status as a bona fide Olympic sport, interest in soccer took off like a comet. Its popularity became so widespread that in 1904 the *Federation Internationale de Football Association* (FIFA), the international governing body of soccer, was formed, part of its duties being to coordinate international matches.

In the early years of Olympic soccer, competition was mostly between European countries, with Great Britain usually the winner. The 1920 Games at Antwerp saw the arrival of two new Olympic participants: Belgium and Czechoslovakia. To everyone's surprise, the young upstarts took over the staring roles, with Belgium defeating Czechoslovakia in the finals.

Oddly enough, while the rest of the world burned with soccer fever, the United States

Photo courtesy of Allsport USA

The Olympic Games bring out the best in players

was slow to embrace the sport, preferring instead its own national pastime: baseball. It wasn't until the 1924 Olympics in Paris that the United States entered its first soccer team. The U.S. team defeated Estonia 1-0 in its first match, but was eliminated by Uruguay 3-0 in the very next round. That year, Uruguay went on to win the world championship.

The 1932 Olympic Games were held in Los Angeles. Since many countries were gripped in economic depression at that time, the cost of transporting an entire soccer team (and its support staff) to North America was out of the question. Therefore, in fairness to everyone, soccer was not on the program for the 1932 Olympics.

In 1936, the Olympics were once again held in Europe, this time in Berlin, Germany. Soccer was restored to the program and after an eight-year absence, fans enthusiastically greeted its return. The United States team showed definite class and a marked improvement in skill. The U.S. team was ultimately defeated by Italy, but it was a close match, with both teams exhibiting extremely good defense. Italy won by a score of 1-0, and eventually went on to capture the gold medal. Experts agreed that the U.S. team was stronger than ever before and might have

Soccer enthusiasm in Latin America

been good enough for a second or third place finish had it not drawn the eventual winner in the very first round. That was the first time an American team had received such recognition.

By 1948, Americans' interest in soccer had widened considerably. More than 5,000 soccer players participated in the pre-Olympic trials and many people believed the 1948 Games in London gave the United States its best chance ever to win a medal. Unfortunately, the U. S. team was eliminated in an early round, but spirits were not dampened; and the team embarked on a post-Olympic, good-will tour, playing Ireland, Norway, and Israel.

Following the 1948 Olympics, interest in soccer rose to greater heights than ever before, particularly in Latin America. Soccer championships and international competitions became so important to the Latin American people that the world's largest stadium was built in Rio de Janeiro, Brazil, just in time for the 1950 World Cup. This stadium, one-half mile in circumference, held the record-breaking crowd of 199,855 people for the final game. It was during this competition that the United States soccer team stunned the world with a 1-0 victory over England.

With so much of the world playing soccer, its future in the Olympics is secure; and every year new countries and new teams test the waters of international competition. In fact, participation has become so extensive that preliminary qualifying and elimination rounds are held on a continental basis. These qualifying to compete against (and learn from) the more experienced teams on each continent.

In addition to adding new countries into the international "family" of soccer, some changes affect new opportunities for those countries already involved in international competition. One major rule change in effect for the 1996 Olympiad in Atlanta, Georgia, will be the addition of women's soccer. This is exciting news for players and fans alike; and gives women all over the world an opportunity to realize their dreams of participating in the world's most prestigious amateur sports competition: the Olympics. By the way, soccer experts already consider the U. S. Women's Team a favorite for a medal in 1996.

Olympic Soccer Winners

1908	1. Britain	1960	1. Yugoslavia
	2. Denmark		2. Demmark
	3. Holland		3. Hungary
1912	1. Britain	1968	1. Hungary
	2. Denmark		2. Bulgaria
	3. Holland		3. Japan
1920	1. Belgium	1972	1. Poland
	2. Spain		2. Hungary
	3. Italy		3. E. Germany
1924	1. Uruguay	1976	1. E. Germany
	2. Switzerland		2. Poland
	3. Sweden		3. USSR
1928	1. Uruguay	1980	1. Czechoslovakia
	2. Argentina		2. E. Germany
	3. Italy		3. USSR
1936	1. Italy	1984	1. France
	2. Austria		2. Brazil
	3. Norway		3. Yugoslavia
1948	1. Sweden	1988	1. USSR
	2. Yugoslavia		2. Brazil
	3. Denmark		3. W. Germany
1956	1. USSR	1992	1. Spain
	2. Yugoslavia		2. Poland
	3. Bulgaria		3. Ghana

THE WORLD CUP

There is little argument that the World Cup of soccer is one of the pinnacles of the world's sporting calendar. Indeed, it has reached a peak alongside that of the Olympic Games in terms of prestige, excitement and international interest. Soccer's influence is ever widening, reaching into the furthest corners of the globe. More or less, wherever a television aerial, radio antenna, or cable link can be accessed, viewers and listeners will be there, enthusiastically supporting the team that represents their country, plays the most exciting game, or simply stirs their emotions.

Since 1974, one major goal of the *Federation Internationale de Football Association* (FIFA), has been to expand interest and participation. Originally, when the tournament began in 1930, there were only 16 teams, but starting with the 1982 World Cup in Spain, the number of finalists was increased to 24. Since expansion would allow more teams to participate, the 1982 ruling was greeted heartily by fans worldwide and has remained in force ever since. Expansion was especially beneficial to those countries where soccer was not yet well established and players were not as experienced. Without expansion it would have been more difficult for newly formed teams to qualify for and participate in World Cup competition.

FIFA has been enormously successful in their efforts to encourage more nations to compete. Today, for example, Africa is guaranteed three spots, while Asia, North America, Central America, and the Caribbean are guaranteed two spots each. The 1994 World Cup was composed of 24 nations: the host team (USA), the defending champion (Germany), and 22 qualifiers. It has been a long road for these teams, a road that started with over 141 nations participating in almost 2 years of qualifying competitions.

History

FIFA was founded in 1904 by six original member countries: Belgium, Denmark, France,

Germany, the Netherlands, and Switzerland. The intent of the international governing body

Photo courtesy of Allsport USA

USA's Ernie Stewart scores winning goal against Columbia in 1994 World Cup.

was to establish a universal set of rules and, under FIFA's guidelines, promote the growth and development of soccer worldwide. In spite of FIFA's good intentions, however, the international sporting press continued to focus its attention on the Olympics. Olympic Games were so popular and garnered so much media exposure that many fans, especially in the United States, thought the Olympics were

---

World Cup Groupings, 1994

GROUP A
1. United States
2. Switzerland
3. Colombia
4. Romania

GROUP B
1. Brazil
2. Russia
3. Cameroon
4. Sweden

GROUP C
1. Germany
2. Bolivia
3. Spain
4. South Korea

GROUP D
1. Argentina
2. Greece
3. Nigeria
4. Bulgaria

GROUP E
1. Italy
2. Ireland
3. Norway
4. Mexico

GROUP F
1. Belgium
2. Morocco
3. Netherlands
4. Saudi Arabia

responsible for soccer's development. FIFA members felt something had to be done to reestablish FIFA's image as the bona fide leader of international soccer. To that end, the members began laying the groundwork for what was to become one of the globe's most prestigious international sports competitions—the World Cup of soccer.

The World Cup has undergone various changes over the years, most notably in how the finalists were selected. Would it be on a straight knock-out basis as was the case in Italy in 1934 and in France in 1938? Or would it be a pool-system producing semi-finalists as it was in the inaugural event? In 1950, when the World Cup was revived following World War II, it reverted to the pool-system, but with the addition of the four winners then playing in a final pool. Eventually, quarter-finals were added along with semi-finals, with the winners going on to compete in the finals and the runners-up competing among themselves for third and fourth places. Soccer was getting so competitive that it was an honor just to make it into the playoffs.

Cup Winners

Year	Location	Champion	Runner-up
1930	Uruguay	Uruguay	Argentina
1934	Italy	Italy	Czechoslovakia
1938	France	Italy	Hungary
1942	[World Cup postponed due to World War II]		
1946	[World Cup postponed due to World War II]		
1950	Brazil	Uruguay	Brazil
1954	Switzerland	W. Germany	Hungary
1958	Sweden	Brazil	Sweden
1962	Chile	Brazil	Czechoslovakia
1966	England	England	W. Germany
1970	Mexico	Brazil	Italy
1974	W. Germany	W. Germany	Netherlands
1978	Argentina	Argentina	Netherlands
1982	Spain	Italy	W. Germany
1986	Mexico	Argentina	W. Germany
1990	Italy	W. Germany	Argentina
1994	United States	Brazil	Italy

World Cup Trophy

After years of careful planning, the first World Cup competition was scheduled to take place in Uruguay in 1930. Everyone agreed that an award should be given, but no one was sure what it should be or how it should look. French sculptor Abel LaFleur was hired to craft a winner's trophy, and his solid gold creation was magnificent. The design depicted the Greek goddess Victory holding an octagonal cup high over her head, her feet resting on a pedestal of semi-precious stones. This was the original World Cup trophy, although it is perhaps now better known as the Jules Rimet Cup, named after the FIFA president who initiated the World Cup tournament.

Italy hosted and won the World Cup in 1934. Then, in 1938, France was the host country, with Italy once again the victor. As a result of the 1938 win, Italy had the cup in its possession at the outbreak of World War II. Legend has it that the statuette was hidden under a bed somewhere in Italy throughout the war to keep it safe from invading forces.

Having survived World War II, the trophy made its way across the Atlantic when Brazil hosted the 1950 World Cup, the first tournament since 1938. The trophy was displayed at the 1950 World Cup and remained in international circulation until it was stolen from a public display prior to the 1966 World Cup tournament in England. Scotland Yard was called in to investigate, but the hero of the search turned out to be a mongrel dog named "Pickles" who uncovered the trophy in a trash heap outside of London!

The trophy returned to service and made several trips across the Atlantic before being retired by Brazil in 1970, the only three-time World Cup winner. Retirement was short lived, however, since the trophy was stolen again in 1973. Unfortunately, this time there was no recovery for LaFleur's beautiful creation. Brazilian authorities discovered that the criminals had melted the trophy for its gold. The Brazilian Football Association replaced it with a duplicate.

The present-day World Cup trophy was donated by FIFA for the 1974 tournament. After studying 53 designs, Italian sculptor Silvio Gazzaniga created the 18 carat solid gold trophy which he describes as follows: "The lines spring out of the base, rising in spirals, stretching out to receive the world. From the remarkable dynamic tensions of the body of the sculpture rise the figures of two athletes at the stirring moment of victory." The current trophy is 14 inches tall and weighs 11 pounds. FIFA retains permanent possession of the new trophy — the World Cup winner takes home a gold-plated replica.

Logo and Mascot, 1994

In the summer of 1990, World Cup USA began a competitive search for a symbol to represent the 1994 World Cup soccer championships. The winning design was created by Pentagram Design, an internationally renowned design firm in New York City. The official logo was unveiled April 17, 1991, and contains a blend of symbols which say "America" and "soccer" in one eye-catching glance.

The logo combines an image of the traditional Stars and Stripes along with a dynamic, speeding soccer ball. The symbol dramatically illustrates unity between a soaring soccer ball and a billowing American flag. The soccer ball and the stars and stripes were selected because of their recognizability and popular appeal. In combination, they link soccer with American culture and promote the 1994 World Cup as an international event.

World Cup USA unveiled the official 1994 mascot on January 14, 1992. The mascot, developed by Warner Brothers Animation Studios, is a playful cartoon-character dog who represents youth, vitality and excitement. When first unveiled, the mascot had no name, so World Cup USA and FIFA World Cup sponsors, launched a "Name the Mascot" contest. The campaign was a six week promotion, drawing more than 25,000 entries. The winning name was STRIKER. In soccer terms, a striker is a player who can always be counted on to take the ball, score a goal, and excite the crowd. And that aptly describes the spirit of the 1994 mascot.

World Cup, 1994

On July 4, 1988, FIFA awarded its prize event to the United States of America for the first time in history. World Cup USA took place from June 17 to July 17, 1994, with the games being played in nine different U.S. cities from coast to coast. The final was held in the famed Rose Bowl at Pasadena, California.

The 15th World Cup of soccer promised to be filled with history making events, and so it was. For the first time since the World Cup started in 1930, the U.S. team advanced past the first round by winning the third game against the favored Colombians with a 2-1 victory. However, the victory was overshadowed when, Andres Escobar, the Colombian player who accidentally scored the first goal for the U.S., was shot to death several

Photo courtesy of Allsport USA

Brazil, the 1994 World Cup Champions

days later in his own country. The U.S. was then slated to play Brazil, who has already won three World Cup championships, for the second round of competition, which started the direct elimination rounds. The U.S. team put up quite a fight, allowing the Brazilian team to score only 1 goal, but it was enough. The U.S. team was out of the tournament with a 1-0 loss.

The U.S. has only played in three other World Cup tournaments. They were invited to the initial 1930 event and again to the 4th World Cup in 1950 after World War II. The U.S. team finally qualified for the first time to play in the 1990 World Cup of soccer, but lost all three first round games. Showing steady improvement, the U.S. is now one step closer to becoming a major competitor in future World Cup games.

Although there was some concern among foreign nations that Americans were not interested in or simply didn't understand soccer, and would not support the games. As the games approached, World Cup officials reported that all but one location completely sold out within one week of the tickets going on sale.

Officials anticipated a stadium audience of more than 3.6 million, as well as more than

Photo courtesy of Allsport USA

Brazil vs. Italy in the World Cup '94 final game

one billion television viewers worldwide! No doubt about it, soccer is one of the most popular sports of the twentieth century, and looks to continue its domination well into the twenty-first century.

Along with 52 games in nine cities, World Cup USA was surrounded by cultural activities, fan festivals, and a week-long party leading into the July 17 championship game. Nearly one million foreign visitors arrived in the States due to the games and the Americans had been looking forward to hosting their international guests for months in advance.

Two to three months prior to the start of the event, visiting teams and their support personnel arrived in the U.S. to begin their final preparations for the games. To accommodate the athletes and their fans, resorts and hotels, particularly those close to a training field or practice site, were converted into homes-away-from-home. Amusement parks and other places of interest geared up for the heavy tourism that was expected and Americans anxiously waited to learn more about soccer from their experienced guests.

Having the best players in the world visit the United States gave American audiences a chance to see soccer at its prime. In fact, the World Cup could prove to be the catalyst for a whole new era of soccer in the United States.

Just in the last five years Americans have become much more knowledgeable about soccer and a lot of that has to do with World Cup as much as with Olympic competition. As a participation sport, soccer has realized the 20-year-old predictions that it would be big in the U.S. by the 1990s. High school soccer has more than doubled in participants since 1980, and soccer is the only high school sport to show steady growth in the past 20 years. At the college level, more teams now compete in soccer than in football. Much of that growth can be traced directly to US Youth Soccer and its National Affiliate members, especially the American Youth Soccer Organization (AYSO) and Soccer for American Youth (SAY). Now with 15.9 million participants nationwide, U.S. Soccer estimates that one out of six Americans is involved in the family of soccer, most as players, coaches, or officials.

Not only has soccer attracted more players, it has grown by leaps and bounds with parents, schools, sponsors, and all-around fans. Today, soccer fans usually have come from one of three groups: those who played it, those whose kids play it, or those who were exposed to it through their ethnic or cultural heritage. As for the World Cup, it all adds up to a lot of fun for the audiences, unbridled enthusiasm for soccer-playing kids, and for everyone a chance to see the very best soccer players the world has to offer.

Photo courtesy of Allsport USA

Tony Meola and Mike Lapper celebrate the historic victory of the USA over Columbia

3

Equipment & Clothing

Soccer is basically a simple game and has limited equipment requirements. This is especially good news for families with more than one child playing at a time. The ball and soccer shoes, often called *boots*, are the only truly essential piece of playing equipment.

The Soccer Ball

Having your very own soccer ball is part of the fun. That way, you can go outside and practice by yourself.

When choosing a soccer ball, there are two main points to consider: the ball's weight and the ball's circumference—the actual distance around the ball. Make sure you get one that isn't too big for you. An official Olympic or World Cup soccer ball has a maximum weight of 16 ounces and a maximum circumference of 28 inches, a size 5. However, this may be too big for young or physically challenged players. The ball should be neither too heavy in weight nor too large in circumference for the size and ability of the player.

As a rule of thumb, the ball should weigh approximately the same number of ounces as your age. For example, if you are 12 years old, a 12 or 13 ounce ball may be just right for you. Of course, there will always be exceptions, but

Photo courtesy of Phil Stephens Photography

This young player shows intense determination

when choosing a soccer ball, this guide will help get you started. Sizes 3 or 4 are generally good choices for young players.   Do not hesitate to select a slightly larger or smaller ball if it feels more comfortable to you, but it's not a good idea to select a ball that's completely out of your size/weight ratio. It will hamper your playing and ball control ability and is probably not the size ball you will be playing with during an actual game.

While a leather ball is preferred for games, for practice your ball can be made of almost any material. (It is not necessary to spend top dollar on a fancy leather ball or one with an endorsement printed on it.) Your ball should be water-repellent (without stitching) so you can play with it in all types of weather and not have to worry about it getting damaged or wet. If you remember to deflate your ball a little when you're not using it, it will last even longer, but don't forget to fill it up again before you play!

Clothing and Shoes

A comfortable pair of shorts, a T-shirt, knee-high socks, and a pair of athletic shoes are all you really need to get started practicing.

However, if you decide to play on a team, you will probably be required to wear the team's uniform.

An official soccer uniform consists of a jersey, a pair of shorts, shin guards, knee-high socks, and a pair of soccer shoes. The goalkeeper's jersey must be a different color than his/her teammates and must also be a different color than the referee's. (Anyone who viewed the 1994 World Cup games on TV saw goalkeepers wearing a great variety of brightly-colored clothing and hair styles!) To prevent bruising

Photo courtesy of Sandra B. Applegate

The goalkeeper's shirt is a different color than those of his teammates

on the arms, the goalkeeper's jersey should have long sleeves. Goalkeepers are the only players permitted to wear gloves. They are also permitted to wear elbow pads, chest pads, knee pads, and hip pads under their uniform. While these items are optional, many coaches insist on the elbow and chest padding. Male goalkeepers also should wear athletic supporters with a plastic cup to avoid injury. Finally, many goalkeepers wear their pads in practice as well as in games.

The one investment you may want to make is to buy a pair of soccer shoes—not simply for looks, but for safety and performance. Take particular care in choosing your shoes and look at light weight, flexible leather *boots* with additional protective padding at the heel, arch, and Achilles tendon.

The best shoes have molded rubber cleats, because traction is vital in soccer, and a padded tongue over the instep. The shoes should have room for an extra pair of socks, yet should fit comfortably, and not be so loose that your foot slides around inside. If your shoes are too big for you, it's easy to turn your ankle because the shoe is not giving you the support that is needed. A little extra room is fine, but they shouldn't be more than a half size larger than your regular shoes. While you may wish to practice in sneakers, particularly indoors, use your regular shoes when you are with the team outdoors.

Years ago soccer player wore all-cotton socks or the stirrup variety that had to be worn with separate sweat socks. Today, most players are wearing full-footed nylon socks with elastic "top bands" so they will stay up. This is much better than using tape or rubber bands.

If the weather is nippy, you may want to wear long sweat pants over your playing shorts for walk out to the field and the warm up. Unless the weather is extremely cold, you should remove your long pants before you start to play. There are two reasons for this: 1) you can quickly become overheated, which can lead to dehydration and fatigue; and 2) you need to be able to move quickly and easily around the field, and that's harder to do when you're all wrapped up!

When you are through playing, put your sweat pants back on so that you don't cool down too quickly. You don't want to expose warm muscles to cold, damp air. Especially on cool

Photo courtesy of Phil Stephens Photography

Shinguards help protect a player's legs

or windy days having a pair of sweats handy can be very beneficial.

Another good investment is a pair of shin guards. During a game, or even during a vigorous practice, you could be accidentally kicked in the shin or around the ankle. Shin guards are sensible protection and should be worn every time you play. (Many coaches will insist that you do.)

If you get in the habit of making them part of your routine, pretty soon you won't even know you're wearing them—but if you get kicked, you'll sure be glad you are.

Photo courtesy of Allsport USA

4

FUNDAMENTALS

Soccer is governed by the same basic set of rules throughout the world, thereby making international games exciting and understandable to spectators from all countries. The objective behind all soccer rules is to keep the game safe, fair, and fun for everyone.

The Field

Soccer is a game played by two opposing teams on a field approximately the size of a football field. (In the United States, smaller fields may be used for very young or physically challenged players.) The measurements of an official soccer field are: minimum length 100 yards, maximum length 130 yards; minimum width 50 yards, maximum width 100 yards.

Goal cages (called goals) are located at each end of the field. Official goals are eight feet

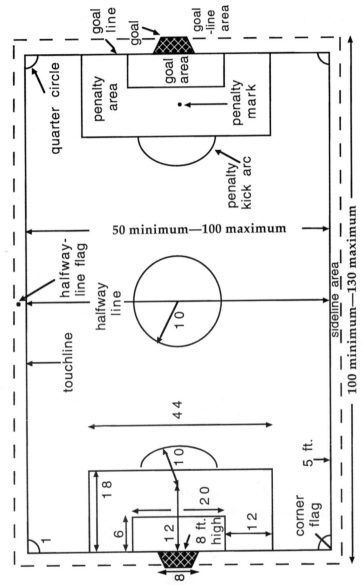

The Soccer Field
(All undesignated distances in yards)

high, 24 feet wide. The depth of the goal is irrelevant since once the ball has completely crossed the goal line, a point has been scored. The ball does not have to touch the back of the goal net.

Flags, called **corner flags,** are located at each of the four corners. There may be two optional flags, one on each side of the field at the halfway line, one yard off of the field. A ball hitting a corner flag, yet remaining in the field, is considered a live ball and is still in play. Flags are not to be removed at any time during the game.

Before a game, the playing field is marked off with chalk. These are **field markings**.

The **center line** divides the field into two halves and is used for kickoffs.

The **touchlines** (sidelines) run the length of the field along each side and form the boundaries for the ball being in play. If the entire ball crosses over the touchline it is considered out of bounds and is put back in play at the place were it went out.

The **goal lines** form the boundaries along the ends of the field. The ball must pass completely over the goal line and into the goal for a goal to be scored.

The **goal area** indicates ball placement territory most apt to facilitate accurate goal kicks.

The **penalty area**, which also includes the goal area, is the territory in which the goalkeeper may handle the ball. On kicks by the defense, the ball must leave the penalty area before being playable by offensive players. Direct free kicks in the penalty area against the defense result in penalty kicks taken from the penalty spot.

The **penalty kick arc** is meant to keep players at least ten yards from the ball when taking penalty kicks. Added in 1937, the penalty kick arc is the most recent change to the soccer field.

The **center circle** is the restraining area for all defensive players on any kickoff.

Once the field has been marked, the goals and corner flags are put in place. The field is now ready for a game to be played. No other field equipment is necessary.

The referee is the official timekeeper. A game clock, scoreboard and/or message board may be displayed for the spectators' enjoyment, but none are required.

The Officials

The head official is called the **referee**. The referee operates inside the playing field, moving along with the action. The referee is assisted by two **linespersons** who operate outside the playing field, moving laterally up and down the touchlines (sidelines). Each

Photo courtesy of AYSO

Referee going over the rules

linesperson carries a white (or yellow-orange), handheld flag. This flag is used by the linesperson to signal balls out of bounds, offsides, and infractions not seen by the referee.

The referee does not carry a flag but uses his hands and arms to signal calls. The referee also has the authority to cite players for personal fouls. The referee carries two pocket-sized cards, one yellow, one red. To indicate which player is being cited, the referee holds up one of the cards. The yellow card signals a warning (called an official caution), but the player being warned may remain in the game. The red card signals a player's ejection from the game. A player who has been ejected cannot be replaced, and the team must play the rest of the game with less than a full squad of 11 players on the field.

The Team

A soccer team has 11 players on the field at any one time; however, a team can, and usually does, have more than 11 members. This makes it possible to substitute one player for another when necessary. In official soccer games governed by the FIFA, only two substitutions are allowed during a game and a player who has gone out may not reenter the game. (In the United States, colleges, high schools, and youth leagues allow a player to reenter.)

Each of the 11 positions is located at a different point on the soccer field, but players may roam as needed during a game. The basic positions are: the goalkeeper, the defenders, the midfielders, and the forwards. Let's look at each in more detail.

Photo courtesy of AYSO

Good ball handling is important

The **goalkeeper** patrols the penalty area and tries to prevent the ball from going into the goal, thereby stopping the opposing team from scoring. The goalkeeper is the only player who may use his/her hands to play the ball.

The **defenders**, also called fullbacks, are positioned directly in front of the goalkeeper. Their primary duty is to prevent the opponent from having a good shot at the goal. The defenders also work to gain possession of the ball and pass it to a teammate to start an attack (offensive play).

The **midfielders**, also called halfbacks, play a transitional game from defense to offense and vice versa. Midfielders have the dual responsibilities of forming their own attacks and upsetting the opponent's attacks. When the opponent has the ball, midfielders can either play a one-on-one coverage or a zone coverage, putting themselves between the ball and the goal cage. When a midfielder gains possession of the ball, he/she should start an offensive attack by passing to another midfielder or a forward.

The **forwards** are the players most responsible for scoring goals. They can also assist with defensive plays by taking the ball away from opposing players. There are two kinds of forwards: *wings* and *strikers*. Wings play towards the outside of the field and work the ball inward to a striker. Strikers play in the middle of the forward line. A striker's primary job is to score goals and he/she must be prepared to shoot upon receiving the ball.

The Game

In soccer, the main objective is to get the ball inside your opponent's goal, while preventing the opponent from getting the ball inside your goal. Goals count one point each. At the end of the game, the team that has scored the most goals wins. To accomplish this objective, the 11 team players assume different positions on the field, yet each player may assume more than one job. Depending on which team has the ball, the same player may be defending or attacking. (In that sense, a soccer team is different from a football team which has a defensive squad and an offensive squad, and both would not be on the field at the same time.)

During a game, players on the same team use a variety of techniques to move the ball toward

Photo courtesy of Phil Stephens Photography

The forward is on the attack

the opponent's goal with the intent of scoring a goal. When the team gets close enough, they will shoot the ball into the goal cage. To score, the ball has to pass between the goal posts and under the crossbar. In order to score, the entire ball must pass over the goal line, but once it has done so, it need not travel any further. It does not have to touch the back of the goal net for the score to count.

An attack (offensive play) can begin any time a team has possession of the ball. The goal-keeper may start an attack by kicking or throwing the ball to a teammate. They, in turn, work the ball toward the opponent's goal, passing the ball to the forwards as they advance. The forwards pass the ball to each other until one sees an opportunity to shoot and, hopefully, score a goal.

A team plays defense anytime the opponent has possession of the ball. When playing defense, the two main objectives are to intercept the ball and keep the opponent from scoring. If the opposing team tries to score, the goalkeeper's job is to stop the ball from going into the goal.

The goalkeeper is the only player who may use his/her hands to play the ball.

As you can see, soccer is definitely a team sport and the entire team should work together at all times both to score and to defend.

Basic Techniques

Soccer players use a variety of techniques to move the ball and score goals. Although skillful players eventually develop their own style, the game is played by using one or more of seven basic techniques: kicking, heading, shooting, trapping, dribbling, tackling, and passing.

Kicking is the technique most often used to move the ball from one teammate to another or to score goals. Accuracy is the key to successful kicking and good players spend hours practicing their technique. If all your kicks go wild, you won't be able to pass

Photo courtesy of Sandra B. Applegate

"Heading" the ball

effectively and the ball will be more apt to go to an opponent than to a teammate!

Heading refers to hitting the ball with your forehead. Heading is an important technique in soccer and can be used to stop the ball, change its direction, or even score a goal. Keep your eyes open and "look" the ball right into your forehead. The key to successful heading is to jump off the ground and actively hit the ball—do not let the ball hit you.

Shooting scores goals and can be done either by kicking or by heading. The most important skills to develop as a shooter are power and accuracy. If the ball is kicked accurately, but with no power, the goalkeeper can easily catch it or knock it away. If the ball is kicked with power but not accuracy, it will simply sail out of bounds.

Trapping is a means of stopping the ball either in flight or on the ground. There are three basic techniques used in trapping: 1) allow the ball to hit your chest at an angle that deflects the ball to the ground, 2) allow the ball to hit your thigh or the side of your bent knee, or 3) use your foot to stop the ball. Once the ball is under your control, you can advance the ball either by dribbling or by passing it on to a teammate.

Dribbling is one technique a player may use to transport the ball from one area of the field to another. Players dribble the ball with their feet, using light taps on the ball to move it along the ground. You must learn to run and dribble in such a way that you do not accidentally overrun the ball, or kick it too far out in front of you. Either situation could allow an opposing player to take possession.

Tackling is the most commonly used technique for getting the ball away from an opponent. Tackling is done only with the feet, never with the hands, and should be done without tripping or kicking your opponent. Good tackling requires lots of practice.

Passing is kicking, pushing, or heading the ball accurately to a teammate or to an open space where a teammate can intercept the ball. Depending on the situation, you may choose to pass the ball along the ground or the air, whichever you feel would be most advantageous for your team.

While it is true that Olympic level and World Cup players spend hours perfecting their skills, anyone and everyone can play just for fun. Players are not limited by physical size or athletic ability. You don't need a lot of equipment and the exercise you will get playing soccer is a benefit in itself.

5

THE 17 LAWS
OF SOCCER

To fully enjoy watching or playing soccer, it helps to have a basic understanding of the rules of the game. In soccer, the rules are called the "laws" and the same laws are used to govern soccer games throughout the world. This makes it easier for spectators and players alike. When games are played between two different countries, everybody uses and understands the same set of laws.

There are only a few exceptions to the international soccer laws in the United States. Youth and physically challenged players may use a lighter ball and a smaller field. They may reenter the game after a substitution and, depending on their physical ability, the game may be less than 90 minutes.

The official text of soccer laws, along with decisions of the International Football Association Board, is available in *Laws of the Game and Universal Guide for Referees* published annually by the *Federation Internationale de Football Association* (FIFA), and reprinted by the United States Soccer Federation (USSF). The laws of soccer are carefully examined each year and changes are made as needed.

The following is a brief summary of the laws—

Law 1: The Field

The diagram in Chapter 5 illustrates the markings for an official playing field. Marking the field with chalk allows players, officials, and spectators to see the boundary lines. The dimensions of an adult field are a minimum 50 yard wide by 100 yards in length to 80 yards by 130 yards.

For youth matches the size of the field may vary: under 12 years (minimum 40 by 80 yards to a maximum 60 by 100 yards, goal 6' high by 21' wide); under 10 years (minimum 40 by 80 yards to a maximum 50 by 90 yards, goal 6' high by 15' wide); under 8 years (minimum 35 by 50 yards to a maximum 50 by 70 yards, goal 6' high by 15' wide).

Law 2: The Ball

The ball should be made of leather or other safe material. Maximum sized balls, known as #5 balls, are 27-28 inches in circumference and 14-16 ounces in weight.

Law 3: Number of Players

Soccer is played with 11 players, including the goalkeeper. Any player on the field may change with the goalkeeper, provided the referee is notified and the change takes place when play is stopped. The number of substitutes may vary, in international competition no more than two are allowed; however, in other matches up to five may be agreed upon by the two teams. A substitute may enter the field only when the referee allows it, and a player who has been "sent off" (ejected) may not be replaced.

Law 4: Players' Equipment

Players must wear a jersey or shirt, shorts, socks and shoes—shin guards may be required in youth play and should be worn by all players. Nothing can be worn which could be considered dangerous to another player. The goalkeeper's shirt must be different than all other players and different than the referee's.

Law 5: Referees

The referee is the ultimate authority before, during, and after a game. The referee's chief responsibilities are to enforce the laws and to make the game as enjoyable, fair and safe for the players as possible. The referee is empowered to call and enforce penalties and is the final authority on determining whether a goal has been scored. He is also the timekeeper.

Photo courtesy of AYSO

A coin toss is used to determine first possession

Law 6: Linespersons

The linespersons provide assistance to the referee by helping to control the game. Their primary duties are to signal when a ball has gone out of play, to indicate which team gets possession, to keep track of substitutions, and to call offside infractions.

Law 7: Duration of the Game

In adult soccer, the game is divided into two periods of 45 minutes each. In the United States, youth soccer and games for physically challenged players are often shorter.

For players *Under 16* (two 40 minute halves; overtime, two 15 minute halves); *under 14 years* (two 35 minute halves; overtime, two 10 minute halves); *under 12 years* (two 30 minute halves; overtime, two 10 minute halves); *under 10 years* (two 25 minute halves; overtime, two 10 minute halves); and *under 8 years* (two 25 minute halves; overtime, two 5 minute halves).

Law 8: Start of Play

The game is started at midfield at the beginning of the game, after a goal has been scored, and after half-time. The ball must be kicked forward, and must travel a distance equal to its circumference before it can be played again.

At the beginning of the game, a coin toss determines which team chooses to kick off first or to select which to defend. When restarting play—stopped when the ball was in bounds—the referee drops the ball where play was stopped, and it is in play when it touches the ground.

Law 9: Ball In and Out of Play

The ball is out of play when it has completely crossed the touchline or the goal line, either in the air or on the ground, or when the game has been stopped by the referee. It is in play at all other times.

Law 10: Scoring

For a goal to be scored, the ball must go completely over the goal line, traveling between the posts and under the crossbar.

Law 11: Offside

A player must not be ahead of the ball when the ball is played by a teammate in his/her direction unless two or more opponents are ahead of him/her. A player cannot be offside when in their own half of the field, or if the player receives the ball from a throw in, goal kick, or corner kick. If a player from the other team plays the ball to you, you cannot be considered offside. The offside is judged at the moment the ball is played.

Law 12: Fouls and Misconduct

This law guides the fair conduct of the game and shows which actions are not allowed. Unless otherwise prohibited and so stated in Law 12, an action is considered fair. The offenses listed below are considered *intentional fouls* and result in a "direct free kick" for the team that was fouled. In a direct free kick, the ball can be kicked directly into the opponent's goal.

Photo courtesy of Allsport USA

This is an intentional foul against a U.S. player

Fouls which result in a Direct Free Kick:

- Kicking or attempting to kick an opponent
- Tripping an opponent
- Jumping at an opponent
- Charging an opponent from behind (unless the opponent is obstructing)
- Charging an opponent in a violent or dangerous manner
- Striking, attempting to strike, or spitting at an opponent
- Holding or pushing an opponent
- Using hands on the ball (except the goalkeeper)

Not all fouls result in a direct free kick. Any of the following result in an "indirect free kick" for the team that was fouled. In an indirect free kick, the ball must be touched by another player from either team before going into the goal.

Fouls which result in an Indirect Free Kick:

- Dangerous play
- Charging fairly, but when the ball is not within range

- Obstructing an opponent
- Charging the goalkeeper
- When a goalkeeper takes more than four steps while holding the ball, delays the game, or has touched the ball when it was deliberately kicked by a teammate.

The remainder of the laws govern the conduct of the players toward each other, the spectators, and the officials. If a player is guilty of violent conduct or serious foul play, or if a player uses foul or abusive language, he/she may be ejected from the game and may not reenter.

Warnings and Ejections:

- Repeated misconduct after a caution
- Entering or leaving the field without the referee's permission
- Disagreeing with the referee
- Unsportsmanlike conduct toward anyone

Law 13: Free Kicks

There are two kinds of free kicks: *direct* and *indirect*. When either of these kicks are taken, all opposing players must stay at least 10 yards away from the ball. When an indirect kick is taken, the referee will raise his/her arm and leave it raised until a second player touches the ball. For a kick to be valid, the ball must be placed at the point of infraction, must not be rolling when kicked, and must travel the length of its circumference before being touched by another player. If the foul resulting in an indirect free kick takes place within the penalty area, the opponents can be less than 10 yards from the ball as long as they are standing on their own goal line between the posts.

Law 14: Penalty Kicks

A penalty kick is awarded when a defending player commits a foul which results in a direct free kick inside his/her own penalty area (see Law 12). A penalty kick is taken from the penalty mark. All players except the kicker and goalkeeper must stand outside the penalty area, at least 10 yards from the penalty mark. The kicker may not play the ball again until it has been touched by another player.

The goalkeeper must stand on the goal line, without moving his/her feet, until after the ball has been kicked.

Law 15: Throw-In

When the ball completely crosses the touchline, the opponent of the team that last touched the ball executes a throw-in at the spot where it went out. The thrower must keep both hands on the ball, throwing it from behind and over his/her head. The thrower must be facing the field, and both feet must be on the ground, either behind or on the touchline. A goal may not be scored directly from a throw-in.

Law 16: Goal Kicks

When the attacking team sends the ball over the goal line, the defending team is awarded a goal kick. Any member of the defending team may take the goal kick. The kicker must send the ball out of the penalty area, and another player must field the ball before the kicker can play it again. No opponents may be in the penalty area when the kick is taken, and no goal can be scored directly from a goal kick.

Law 17: Corner Kicks

When the defending team sends the ball over the goal line, the attacking team retains possession with a kick from the quarter circle by the corner flag closest to where the ball went out. The flag cannot be moved and opponents must remain at least 10 yards away until the ball travels its circumference. Another player must field the ball before the kicker can play it again.

A goal may be scored directly from a corner kick.

* * * * *

For more detailed information on the laws, as well as information on the duties of the referee and linespersons, consult a current issue of *Laws of the Game* published by FIFA, available in the U.S. through the United States Soccer Federation, 1801-1811 S. Prairie Ave, Chicago, IL 60616.

Photo courtesy of Sandra B. Applegate

6

GUIDELINES FOR PLAYERS & SPECTATORS

There is a wealth of soccer activity now available in many communities, ranging from youth programs on up through visiting international teams. The chances are that you and your family are learning about soccer together, so now would be a good time to attend some games and see what the excitement is all about.

The skill and athleticism of semi-professional or professional soccer teams is a feat to behold, and can be a real inspiration to youth and amateur soccer players of every age and level of skill.

Tips From the Pros

Listed below are some tips from the pros. When you watch a soccer game, look for these techniques in action. If you play soccer yourself, you may want to develop some of these skills in your own game:

- Experienced players run even when they don't have the ball. They are always trying to create openings where they can receive passes or open up a lane for a teammate who does have the ball.

- Pros don't stop when they've been fouled—they keep right on playing and let the referee be the one to control the game.

- When two players are going for the ball, the others will wait at a distance, ready to receive a pass or intercept a "stray" ball. They do not "gang up" around the ball for this leaves the field unprotected with no one available to receive a pass and advance the ball.

- Throw-ins are taken by the player nearest the ball.

- If an opening comes up on the field, a player will quickly move into that opening, ready to receive a pass or defend against an attack.

- Even the best players have only a few truly superior moves, but they do them well, and with either foot. This comes from practice, practice, practice—the pros know you've got to master the basics first.

Watch for certain players to demonstrate their "speciality" and see how consistent they are with its execution. If you play soccer, don't worry about trying to be good at everything at once. Take a tip from the pros, practice the basics—get them down and the rest will follow.

- Pros take care of their health. They eat right and get enough rest so that they can play with energy and gusto. They also know the benefit of mental discipline and keep their minds on the game at all times. It's easy to get distracted at a big game because there is a lot going on everywhere. Watch a pro player when he's on the bench. His eyes and thoughts are on the game. That takes self-discipline and determination.

- Pros do a lot of talking to each other on the field. They advise teammates of field position, warn each other of an impending tackle, call out for the ball if they are open, and freely extend congratulations, encouragement, and moral support. They do not, however, waste energy criticizing each other, the opponents, or the officials. That's negative behavior, and they know that negative behavior can be defeating.

The Importance of Teamwork

Soccer is, above all, a team sport. In order for a team to work well together, every player must be allowed and encouraged to contribute to the best of his/her ability. When you watch a soccer game, either in person or on television, watch for the interplay between teammates.

With 11 members on the field, no one player ever determines whether a team wins, and no one player should ever be made to feel responsible for a loss.

It is important for players to feel good about each other and about the team as a whole. Players should be able to trust each other to show up for games and practices, and to play their best. If your team meets these standards, then you are on your way to becoming a good team that works well together.

If the team is working together, whenever a player gets the ball, he/she will know that the

Photo courtesy of Sandra B. Applegate
Players working out their game plan

rest of the team will be moving into open space for a pass. Successful teams do not have "glory hogs" who want to keep the ball to themselves. Besides, if a player should lose the ball, he/she needs the support and cooperation of teammates to recover and keep the attack going.

No matter what your skill level, there are certain things that you can do to support the team effort:

- Support the efforts of each player no matter what the outcome. No one tries to miss a goal or a tackle. Sometimes the opponent simply has the edge on a certain play. Let your teammate know that you are aware of his/her effort and offer encouragement.

- If someone on your team scores a goal, go over and give him/her your congratulations. If you score a goal, let the player who made the pass to you know how important his/her effort was in helping you score. No one makes a goal without the assistance of his/her teammates!

- If you blame someone for a mistake, it will probably happen again. This is because when we focus on negative behavior, we aren't free to concentrate on the positive. People repeat a "mistake" because it is foremost in their minds. Forget about it and get on with the game. After all, if you make a mistake, do you want teammates and spectators to constantly remind you of it? Probably not. Leave the coaching to the coach. Encouragement reaps more rewards than criticism.

• The best thing you can do for your teammates is simply to try your best and display a positive and supportive attitude. Go to every practice, listen to your coach, and show that you are trying. That's all anyone can ask from you, that's all you should ask from anyone else. Have fun and don't fret about a "mistake," either yours or anyone else's.

Helpful Hints for Spectators

Spectators are a vitally important part of the game, and players enjoy playing before a knowledgeable and appreciative audience. From beginning youth leagues through Olympic and World Cup competitions, the thrill of playing before a live audience brings out the best in every player.

If you and your family are just now getting interested in soccer, or even if you've been at it for quite a while, go watch as many games as you can. You will learn more about the sport by being up close to the action, and the enthusiasm generated by the spectators is infectious—you'll be a soccer fan in no time, if you aren't already! Remember that part of being a "good" fan is to be supportive without interfering in the game itself. At youth soccer games, spectators are not allowed behind the goals. If you're not sure where to stand or sit, ask for directions, and never walk across a playing field when a game is in progress. If you follow these simple spectator guidelines, you'll always be welcome at any soccer game.

When you watch a game, look for certain strategies and techniques to be displayed. Obviously, older, more experienced players will be able to demonstrate a more sophisticated style than will a team of younger players, but the real joy of soccer is in its simplicity. The objective is the same at all levels: to score goals. How artfully those goals are scored is only a matter of degrees.

Part of the appeal of soccer is expecting the "unexpected." You never know who's going to have the ball when, or what will happen. The continuous interplay between offense and defense, the various techniques a player may use, and the change of pace within the game make for a very stimulating experience. In fact, spectators have been known to get so involved rooting for their team that when the game is over they are as tired as the players!

It happened at the 1968 Olympic Games in Mexico City. In spite of the fans' effort to cheer on the home team, Mexico did not make the finals. No matter, the crowd exerted just as much effort cheering on the gold and silver medal teams, Hungary and Bulgaria, respectively. Japan took the bronze medal and Mexico finished fourth. No matches were held to determine the rankings of the quarterfinal losers. By that time, the audience was too exhausted and worn down to concern itself with any further consolation games. Everyone was hoarse from cheering and rooting. Indeed, spectators are a vital part of soccer.

Soccer Parents' Code of Conduct

It's very important for children to feel that their parents applaud them and take an interest in their activities. Stress the positive, not the negative. Cheer for the other players on your child's team (and reward a fine play by the opposing team as well). Your child will respond to your sense of fair play and appreciate your awareness of the game. Children emulate the behavior they see in other people, especially their parents. By receiving support and encouragement from their parents, they learn to be supportive of their teammates and coaches and respectful to officials and opponents.

Photo courtesy of Phil Stephens Photography

Children develop confidence playing soccer

The most important benefits to children playing soccer are that not only are they involved in an exciting sport, they are also developing confidence and self-esteem—valuable assets that will serve them well throughout childhood and into adulthood.

The best way to help a child achieve goals and reduce the natural fear of failure is through positive reinforcement. No one likes to make a mistake. If your child does make one or two, so what—remember, he or she is still learning. Encourage your child's efforts and point out the good things done well that day, both on and off the field. As long as children give their best, they deserve to be treated as winners.

7

First Aid & Safety

Soccer is a contact sport, played often at full speed where collisions can result in an injury. Most players will encounter their share of bumps and bruises.

Fortunately, most soccer-related injuries—especially those involving young athletes—are not serious, *but the best rule is to never take a chance with an injured player.*

The following guidelines will help you deal successfully with an injury on the field:

- ***Always Remain Calm.*** The injured player's recovery may depend on the decisions you make on the field, and it's hard to make accurate decisions when you're flustered. Moreover, your behavior may determine the reactions of others around you, including players, parents, and spectators, and no one will be served by people running around screaming.

- ***Never Assume the Role of a Physician***. Whenever there is any doubt as to the nature or extent of an injury, refer the injured player to a physician.

- ***Never Move a Player Who May Have a Serious Injury.*** Resist the urge to move an injured player to a more comfortable location (such as under a shade tree or into the locker room). Moving an injured player could compound the injury. Do not encourage the player to "sit up" or to rise from the field. Call for emergency assistance (fire, police, etc.) whenever you are in doubt about an injury. Remember, it's always better to be safe than sorry.

Photo courtesy of Allsport USA

Injuries can happen when playing soccer

The First Aid Kit

It's a good idea to keep a basic first aid kit on hand at all times. Many pharmacies and sporting goods stores carry well-stocked first aid kits that would be fine for soccer. If you want to put one together yourself, the following items should be included:

- Adhesive tape of various sizes

- Adhesive bandages of various shapes and sizes

- Ammonia caps (for dizziness)

- Antiseptic soap (for washing a wounded area)

- Antiseptic solution (bug bites, minor scrapes)

- Aspirin or equivalent for simple headaches (for youth teams, no medication should be disbursed without written parental permission, signed and dated, authorizing the disbursement of aspirin, etc.)

- Blanket to cover injured player (warmth reduces chance of shock)

- Cold packs

- Elastic wraps of various sizes

- Eyewash solution

- Gauze pads

- Hank's solution (trade name Save-a-tooth)

- Plastic bottle filled with fresh water

- Sterile cotton sheets (can be cut to fit)

- Scissors

- Tissues and pre-moistened toweletts

- Tweezers (for splinters)

The phone number of the nearest ambulance service should be taped to the inside of your first aid kit, along with a reminder that you can always call 9-1-1 in an emergency. All players and coaches should know where the first aid kit will be kept at any practice or game site. The kit does you no good if you can't find it! Make sure someone knows the location of the closest telephone and always keep a quarter or two in the kit so you won't have to hunt for change in an emergency.

Photo courtesy of Sandra B. Applegate

Emergency Care of a Knocked-Out Tooth

Folklore to the contrary, in most case an avulsed (knocked out) tooth can be replanted and retained for life. In fact, research shows that when an avulsed tooth can be replanted within 30 minutes, the success rate for long-term retention is greater than 90 percent. Timing is critical, however, and much depends on the handling of the tooth itself. The three most important considerations are: 1) length of time out of the socket, 2) storage medium, and 3) transportation mechanism.

In years past, whenever a tooth was knocked out, the common practice was to wrap the tooth in tissue or gauze, or immerse it in water, sterile saline, saliva, or milk. Although well-intentioned, each of these methods has been shown to have serious drawbacks.

Recently, safer, more effective means of tooth storage and transportation have been developed. The best way to store a tooth is to immerse it in a pH balanced, buffered cell-preserving solution such as Hank's or Viaspan® (used for transplant organ storage). Hank's solution, under the trade name "Save-a-tooth," may be purchased over-the-counter at many drug stores. It provides safe storage for 24-hours and has a shelf life of two years.

With intelligent handling and a proper storage and transport device, an injured athlete has an excellent chance of having an avulsed tooth successfully replanted. Tooth storage and transport containers should be available at every school, camp, social, and athletic event.

Mouthguards

According to the California Dental Association, mouthguards prevent an estimated 200,000 oral injuries to the teeth, lips, cheeks, and gums each year in the United States alone. In addition, properly fitted custom made mouthguards can protect against concussion and head and neck injuries. Custom made mouthguards should not be confused with the common "boil and bite" type bought at sporting goods stores. The custom mouthguard, made by your dentist, is not bulky, does not interfere with breathing, covers all posterior teeth, and fits tightly. You often do not know you are wearing a mouthguard at all. The "boil and bite" mouthguards often do not meet all these criteria.

No matter what sport you play, custom mouthguards can help prevent oral injuries. They are especially important for young children just starting out in sports. In fact, if you get used to wearing one early, it will be easier to continue wearing one at the high school and collegiate levels where competition is more aggressive.

When weighing the costs of a mouth protector (approximately $5.00 for a "boil and bite" to $50.00 for a custom fit) against the costs of repairing a damaged root or tooth ($1,200 - $1,500 per tooth, depending on the circumstances), mouth protectors are the clear winners.

Furthermore, because of blood-born diseases such as hepatitis B and HIV, it is all the more important to decrease the number of bleeding injuries. Rules are now being adapted to remove from the field any player who is bleeding. Mouthguards dramatically reduce the number of bleeding incidents in sports-related accidents.

Bumps, Bruises and Breaks

One problem with playing team sports is that invariably someone will get hurt and once in a while that might be you! Remember, the most important thing to do when a player gets hurt is to stay calm. Next, a decision must be made as to the extent of the injury.

Skin injuries are, of course, visible in the form of abrasions, pinches, cuts, rashes and redness, most of which are easily treated with a petroleum-based antibiotic ointment containing bacitracin or neomycin and an adhesive bandage. Fat injuries are a little harder to see right away. This type of injury is most often seen as minor swelling which may later become a bruise.

Muscles injuries can be considerably more serious. When a muscle is hit with enough force, bleeding usually occurs. Depending on how hard the hit, swelling may be slow (30-60 minutes or more) or quick (5-20 minutes), and tenderness may run the entire length of the muscle. In either event, ice packs are the appropriate treatment, and if the player responds soon, he/she may reenter the game. More serious muscle injuries must be evaluated by a medical doctor.

Joint injuries are often the most difficult to evaluate. Initial treatment of such sprains or tears would be the application of ice, usually in the form of large bags wrapped around the joint. These types of injuries should always have a medical doctor's evaluation.

Broken bones are usually obvious by the severity of the pain, the rapidity of the swelling (within a few minutes), and/or the possibility of the bone protruding from its normal position. The exact site of the fracture can be found by "walking" the fingers along the sore area starting at a point several inches away, then approaching gently until the maximum tenderness is located. Breaks can usually be localized within a half inch area, whereas bruises and sprains are spread over a wider area. Determining location may be more difficult in the hand or foot where there are many small bones, but x-rays can help pinpoint the break.

The question of whether to use ice or heat is one of timing. Initially, ice should be applied since coldness will reduce both swelling and pain. Ice can be applied continuously unless it becomes more uncomfortable than the injury, at which time a fifteen minute rest should be allowed. After two or three days, when the tendency for swelling has slowed or stopped, warm (not hot) soaks can be started along with motion therapy (gentle movement of the afflicted limb). Motion stimulates the healing process by encouraging the growth of new blood vessels, although it may cause a slight increase in swelling temporarily. About 15 to 20 minutes of warm soaking, along with gentle motion, will get the healing process to move along swiftly.

Wrist and Hand Injuries

Injuries to the wrists and hands are common in fast moving sports. Wrists can be sprained or fractured from falls, and fingers can be caught and jammed. Most of these injuries cannot be avoided as they take place during the vigorous action of a game. Certain measures, however, may prevent serious injury. Rings and jewelry, such as bracelets, necklaces and earrings, should always be removed before playing. These objects could catch in clothing resulting in serious cuts, or at the extreme, loss of a finger.

If fingers do get hurt, they need to be protected from further damage. An injured finger with mild swelling can be taped to an adjacent finger for protection. Occasionally, players try to "pop" the joint back into place, thinking the finger is merely dislocated, but sometimes there may be a fracture involved and this could cause long term problems. Even simple dislocations may be complicated by stiffness or recurrent redislocation if not taken care of properly.

Swelling that persists for more than a day or two following injury should be checked by a physician and x-rays taken. If a fracture is missed and allowed to heal for two or three weeks in an incorrect position, permanent deformity may result.

Never neglect an injury to the arm, wrist or hand. These injuries often seem minor but can result in permanent loss of function if not treated. For best results the injury should be identified and treated as soon as possible.

Guidelines for Reducing Injuries

Although no amount of planning and preparation can guarantee that a player will never be injured, there are many things a team can do to protect themselves. These guidelines should be followed to help reduce injuries.

- Inspect the facility and equipment for hazards. Make sure soccer balls are properly inflated and free from snags. Report dangerous conditions to an official and do not play on any field that appears to be unsafe.

- Have a team discussion about the types of injuries that can occur in soccer and remind everyone to keep an eye out for the well-being of teammates and opponents alike.

- Players should always warm up and stretch properly before all practices and games. Officials should warm up too so that they can keep up with the action on the field.

- "Horsing around" is a common cause of injury. Players should observe game rules and practice good sportsmanship at all times.

- In soccer, a player's feet and legs take a lot of stress and are vulnerable to injury. One way to help protect your feet is to always have proper footwear. You can prevent blisters by wearing shoes and socks that fit correctly, by gradually breaking in new shoes, and by wearing an extra or heavier pair of socks, if necessary. You can help protect your legs by always wearing shin guards.

- Players should not practice or play in a game when hurt or not feeling well. Better to take a few days off and come back strong.

- Carry a first aid kit and always have water available.

- Prevent heat injuries and dehydration by taking regular water breaks and rest periods, in the shade, if possible.

- Always seek prompt medical attention for an injured player. If you do not know what to do, call for emergency assistance immediately. Do not move an injured player, but you may cover him/her with a lightweight blanket. Warmth reduces the chance of an injured person going into shock.

Photo courtesy of World Cup and Lynne Meterparel

Proper stretching is essential to prevent injury

Photo courtesty of World Cup and Lynne Meterparel

More stretching exercises

Parents with active young atheletes will be rewarded by rereading the valuable information in this and the following section and keeping it available—it is not just for soccer!!!

8

HEALTH &
PHYSICAL FITNESS

Young athletes make special demands on their bodies when they play hard—whether soccer, skateboarding or cycling. They should pay attention to the advice their parents and coaches give them regarding proper foods to eat and ways to build strength and agility.

Nutrition

The connection between food, physical fitness, and freedom from disease has been known since written records were begun. In the Far East, the health benefits of foods go back to at least 2600 B.C. In the West, scholars of ancient Greece, around 2500 B.C., were very much aware of the connection between food and health. Ours is not the first society to know that "you are what you eat."

The main nutrition message is simple. Eating a variety of high quality foods of plant origin (vegetables, fruits and cereals) produces the highest quality of health.

Photo courtesy of Sandra B. Applegate

The best part of half time is the tradition of eating oranges

It is not necessary to eat animal products to gain an edge in sports, either in endurance or in strength. In fact, quite the opposite is true and this has been known, but ignored, for most of this century.

Consider, for example, what truly great athletes have discovered. Carl Lewis, winner of the most track and field gold medals in Olympic history; Henry "Hammerin' Hank" Aaron, all-time major league home run champion; Martina Navratilova, ranked as one of the world's top tennis players; Dave Scott, the only person to win the Ironman Triathlon more than twice (6 times!); Robert Parish, 7'0", 260 pound starting center for the Boston Celtics; and Roy Hilligan, winner of the Mr. America body building championship all follow a very low-fat diet, composed almost entirely of plant foods.

Health Hazards

Athletes of all ages, but especially young athletes, are subject to a wide variety of pressures, not the least of which are to "look good and perform well." For some young people, the desire to conform to outside pressures and to meet everyone's expectations (no matter how unrealistic) entices them to attempt desperate, even life-threatening, measures.

Eating Disorders

Society puts enormous pressure on young people, especially young women, to be thin as well as athletic. The young athlete's concern with how she "looks" in her attire, peer pressure to be as thin as a model, plus a misguided belief that weight loss always leads to improved performance all contribute to a growing number of cases of eating disorders. So extreme is this phenomenon that the United States Olympic Committee recently reported that today more people suffer from compulsive eating disorders that threaten good health and, for some, life itself, than at any time in the nation's history. The two most common eating disorders are *bulimia* and *anorexia nervosa* — both are extremely dangerous and can be difficult to treat. An estimated four to five percent of all teenagers and young adult females now suffer from these illnesses!

Bulimia is characterized by alternate cycles of binge eating with restrictive eating and self-induced vomiting. Some also use laxatives and diuretics. Bulimia is addictive in nature.

Anorexia nervosa is characterized by extreme thinness, preoccupation with being overweight, self-imposed starvation, and excessive physical activity. This condition may also be addictive.

Dentists and physicians can screen for these symptoms during pre-season physical examinations, but other players and family members, all of whom spend more time with the athlete than does the dentist or physician, can help by recognizing tell-tale signs. Among those signs to watch for are: the athlete's repeated comments about fear of being fat, excessive weight loss, vomitus odor, frequent complaints of constipation, excessive physical activity, excessive use of laxatives, and absence of at least three menstrual cycles in a row. These symptoms frequently indicate the possible existence of serious eating disorders. If someone you know exhibits one or more of these symptoms and the person is under age, make an effort to alert a parent or guardian; in the case of an adult, encourage her to seek treatment. Eating disorders are serious health hazards and should not be ignored.

Smokeless Tobacco and Tooth Decay

National data surveys, most notably by the Tobacco Intervention Network in Gresham, Oregon, indicate that about 16% of males between 12 and 25 years of age have used some form of smokeless tobacco within the past year, and that from 33% to 50% of that group used smokeless tobacco at least once a week. Some studies have indicated 3% to 8% of children in the seventh grade use smokeless tobacco on a daily basis, increasing to 10% to 15% of those in the twelfth grade. These statistics are alarming in and of themselves, but most alarming were the reasons given for using smokeless tobacco: peer pressure and a desire to be like their "heroes," notably professional athletes.

The health consequences of using smokeless tobacco are numerous. Dental caries (cavities) and periodontal (gum) disease increase as well. Pouch tobacco has an average sugar content of 35%. Anyone could figure out that bathing teeth in such a sugar content will definitely increase the risk of cavities. Furthermore, the gums recede from the tooth surfaces in the immediate area where the tobacco is held, causing gum disease, bone loss, and even tooth loss.

The National Institute of Drug Abuse and the American Psychological Association agree that smokeless tobacco can produce dependency and result in addiction.

There are many side-effects when using smokeless tobacco, among these are an increase in blood pressure, an increase in heart rate, and a higher occurrence of kidney disease. There is absolutely no evidence that smokeless tobacco gives athletes a competitive edge in reaction time, movement time, or total response. There is, however, a good bit of evidence suggesting that the use of smokeless tobacco can rob an athlete of a long life and good health.

Anabolic Steroids

All of us want to be liked. That instinct is as natural as the desire for food or sleep. Yet our craving for the approval of others can sometimes have grave consequences. Certainly that is true in the use of steroid drugs, properly called anabolic-androgenic steroids (AAS).

Why do people take these harmful drugs? Apparently, to improve athletic performance and/or to enhance muscular development, yet the consequences are so horrendous they easily outnumber any possible benefits the user could hope to attain. AAS can cause boys to develop breasts, lose their hair, contract acne or have their skin and eyes turn yellow, among other undesirable results. AAS use by girls can result in permanent deepening of the voice, shrinkage of the breasts, irregular menstrual cycles, and the growth of facial and body hair. In both sexes, body growth can be permanently stunted.

Changes are not limited to the physical. Among the psychological effects of AAS, the American Sports Education Institute includes the following: "Wide mood swings ranging from periods of violent, even homicidal, episodes known as 'roid rages' to depression, paranoid jealousy, extreme irritability, delusions, and impaired judgment." It is difficult to understand why anyone would knowingly court this kind of trouble, but despite all the warnings about the harmful effects of AAS, an estimated one million young men and women continue to use them. The sale of illegal steroids in the

United States alone (largely through gyms or direct mail) has now reached an annual volume estimated at $400 million. Moreover, a sizable percentage of those who use these drugs are not even directly engaged in competitive sports; they simply want to look like Superman or Wonder Woman.

The most widely publicized cases of steroid misuse have often involved star athletes, such as Canadian sprinter Ben Johnson who was stripped of his gold medal in the 100 meter dash following the 1988 Olympics. Four years earlier, cyclist Cindy Olavarri was disqualified from competing in the 1984 Olympics after she tested positive for steroids. After years of AAS use, she found her immune system had been weakened, her ligaments and joints damaged, her liver had become inflamed, and she developed a cancerous back tumor, in addition to other ailments. These cases are by no means unique. Many athletes, particularly weight-lifters, track and field competitors and professional football players, have been caught up in the web of steroid use.

The use of AAS for muscle building or improving athletic performance has been deplored by many national organizations. Among them are the American Medical Association, the International Olympic Committee, the National Collegiate Athletic Association and the National Football League.

To learn more about AAS, the case against steroid use has been cogently summarized by authors James E. Wright and Virginia S. Cowart in their book, *Anabolic Steroids: Altered States* in which they write:

"There is beauty in athletic feats performed with skill and grace. There is pride in seeing athletes achieve higher levels than they ever dreamed they could reach....What we don't want them to become is inhuman."

Sports and Vision

Your vision, just like the strength in your arms and the speed in your legs, is an important part of your overall performance. To play your best, you must know what's behind you, beside you, and in front of you at all times, and this takes a variety of vision skills. If your natural vision is not what you think it should be, you may want to ask your doctor about corrective lenses.

There is now a new impact resistant lens available for prescription glasses that is reasonable in cost, light weight, and will not shatter if broken. Another option is contact lenses, but be sure to bring cleaning and wetting solutions, as well as storage containers, with you to all games and practices, just in case.

Getting a foreign object in the eye is the most common eye problem associated with sports. Foreign objects range from minor irritants such as dust or dirt, to more serious intrusions such as a "poke" in the eye or a blow to the head around the eye. A kicked soccer ball can reach a speed up to 75 mph and is responsible for most soccer-related eye injuries. Due to the high-impact energy of a flying soccer ball, heading the ball should be discouraged, especially among young players.

A blow to the head, especially around the eye, may produce bleeding in or under the skin, causing a "black eye." An ice pack can help reduce swelling. After a week or so, the discoloration will start to fade and eventually disappear. If there is any doubt about the severity of a blow around or directly to an eye, call your eye doctor or go to the nearest emergency room at once. Do not rub, wash, or apply pressure to the eye.

Care of the Eyes

Fortunately, the eye has a number of natural protective mechanisms. It is recessed in a bony socket, the quick-blinking reflexes of the eyelids and eyelashes deflect most foreign particles, and natural tears wash away most minor irritants. If you do get something in your eye, follow these simple guidelines:

- Do not rub your eye or use a dirty cloth or finger to remove the obstruction.

- Irritants can often be eliminated by looking down and pulling the upper eyelid outward and down over the lower lid.

- If you see a particle floating on your eye, you may gently remove it with the corner of a clean piece of cloth.

- Apply an eye wash or tap water to flush out the irritating particle. If the object doesn't wash out, keep the eye closed, bandage lightly and seek emergency professional care.

Warning signs of potentially serious eye problems are: blurring, loss or change in vision, seeing rainbows or halos around lights, seeing flashing lights or shooting stars. Any of these symptoms deserve prompt attention from an eye care professional.

Whatever your recreational activity, your vision plays a vital role in helping you enjoy the sport and perform at peak efficiency. Your eyes are irreplaceable—they deserve the best of care.

Fitness Training

There are many ways to improve your physical fitness and increase your stamina so that you can be your best and have fun while playing soccer. It isn't much fun to play soccer if after only a few minutes you are unable to catch your breath!

Walking, jogging, light weight training, even playing another favorite sport with a friend (like tennis), are all excellent ways to become fit.

Just remember to start slow and don't overdo it. Gradually increase the level of difficulty as well as the amount of time you spend working out. Keep yourself on a regular schedule and eat balanced meals. Soon you will be well on your way to a lifetime of good health.

Photo courtesy of AYSO

Soccer is fun for all ages

9

Youth Soccer

The United States Soccer Federation (USSF) is the national governing body for soccer, and most people commonly refer to it by its new name, US Soccer. Interest in soccer keeps growing and growing all over the world. In fact, there are more than two million registered children—boys and girls—playing in the American Youth Soccer Organization (AYSO), Soccer for American Youth (SAY) and the US Youth Soccer Association (USYSA).

These players, from 8 to 18-years-of-age, participate in regular league play, tournaments, skills clinics, soccerfests and foreign exchanges. Additionally, more skilled players may qualify for the special national youth teams: Under-20, Under-18, Under-17 and Under-16.

Let's take a closer look at what youth soccer has to offer and how you can get involved.

Benefits of Team Sports

One of the best things about soccer is that you don't have to be a "natural-born athlete" to play. Even if you've never played any type of sport before, you can play soccer. That's because the rules are simple and the basic skills—running and kicking the ball—can be picked up by everyone. You don't need experience and you can begin playing at any age.

If you like lots of action and want to meet new friends, there's nothing better than joining a soccer club. As a club member, you'll not only improve your athletic skills and build self-confidence, you'll also learn about teamwork and sportsmanship, and the importance of working with others. You'll challenge yourself to improve your skills and stay physically fit, and best of all have fun doing it.

Don't hesitate to get involved for lack of equipment. For example, if you join the AYSO, they will supply a game ball as well as the jersey, shorts, and socks that make up your soccer uniform. You need only supply your own shoes. (We took a close look at clothing and equipment in Chapter 3, below.)

Team sports are just as important for girls as they are for boys. Unfortunately, people didn't always think so, and that kept girls on the sidelines. Not anymore! Girls are playing sports and enjoying every minute of it, and their parents and friends are behind them all the way.

Photo courtesy of Sandra B. Applegate
Youth soccer means friendship

The American Youth Soccer Organization stresses the following basic philosophies:

- **Everyone Plays:** No one wants to ride the bench. Under AYSO rules, every player participates in at least half of every game. That way no one, regardless of skill level, is left out. The more you play, the better you get, the more fun you have.

- **Balanced Teams:** Every AYSO Region is required to set up teams as evenly balanced as possible. After all, it's more fun to play when teams are of equal ability.

Photo courtesy of AYSO

Parent encouraging young players

- **Open Registration:** Interest and enthusiasm are the only criteria needed to sign up for soccer. Registration is open to all youngsters between the ages of 5 and 18.

- **Positive Coaching:** AYSO coaches are trained and encouraged to make the extra effort to understand and offer players positive help and reinforcement, rather than negative criticism.

- **Good Sportsmanship:** The purpose of youth soccer is to create a positive environment based on mutual respect, rather than a win-at-all-costs attitude. All AYSO programs are designed with an emphasis on good sportsmanship, positive self-esteem, and kindness toward others.

Photo courtesy of AYSO

Team picture day was special for these VIP players

Children With Special Needs

AYSO also has a program to include children with special needs, including physical and developmental handicaps or disabilities. In this program, known as VIP, children can play soccer at their own level, without being overwhelmed by more vigorous players. VIP players make friends, develop self-esteem, and learn that they are a valuable part of a team. Community involvement is an important part of the VIP program and "buddies" are drawn in from other teams to help VIP players, both on and off the field.

Fun Jobs for Volunteers

Soccer is not only a team sport, it's a family sport. Parents and grandparents are encouraged to get involved with their children's soccer program and join the fun. AYSO provides complete training for adult family members who want to be coaches or referees. Adults can also get involved by being a commissioner, treasurer, newsletter editor, or team mom or dad. Volunteers are always needed to help with telephone calls and mailings, car pooling, staffing food stands at the games, marking chalk lines on the playing field, and a variety of other support functions.

Player/Referee Organization

Older brothers and sisters can get involved too. In fact, AYSO offers a training program for children 12-years and older who would like to be officials. This program is called the Player Referee Organization (PRO). Participants get the same training as any AYSO referee and when they have completed their training, they may act as a linesperson in games for their own age level, or as a referee in games for players younger than themselves. Older players are also welcome to coach younger teams. Player/coaches have the advantage of being able to draw from their own playing experience to help young players understand the game. Because they are players themselves, older children who coach understand the youngsters' problems, and can answer questions with a real in-depth knowledge of the game.

As you can see, soccer is one sport that truly offers something for every member of the family.

To find out how you can get involved, contact:

United States Soccer Federation, Inc.,
1801-1811 S. Prairie Ave.,
Chicago, IL 60616

or

American Youth Soccer Organization
5403 W. 138th St.
Hawthorne, CA 90251

10

GLOSSARY

Like all sports, soccer has a lexicon of its own. Being familiar with the language of soccer will help you understand the game (and that will make you a better player). Using official soccer terms to ask a question or explain a situation will facilitate communication among players, coaches and officials alike.

Advantage - If the referee feels that the whistle should not be blown, even though there has been a foul, he/she says, "Play on, advantage!" This means the player or team who was fouled is better off just keeping the ball than getting a free kick.

Caution - A player who disobeys the laws, behaves in an unsportsmanlike manner, disagrees with the referee, or leaves the field without the referee's permission, receives a caution (yellow card) from the referee. A player who repeats the misconduct (after receiving a caution) will be ejected from the game (red card) and cannot be replaced.

Center - A pass that moves the ball from the outside to the center of the playing field.

Center Circle - The circle with the 10 yard radius located in the center of the playing field.

Center Forward - Also called a striker. This is the center player in the offensive attack and usually scores lots of goals.

Charging - Using a shoulder against an opponent's shoulder to gain an advantage. If the ball is within three feet of the players involved, charging is permitted.

Club Linespersons - When no neutral linespersons are available, the referee may appoint two club linespersons to patrol the touchlines and wave a flag when the ball goes out of bounds. This appointment is valid only for the duration of that particular game and does not confer status on the appointees as "officials."

Corner Area - The arc at each corner of the playing field where corner kicks are taken.

Corner Flags - The four flags located in the four corners of the playing field. A ball hitting a corner flag yet remaining on the field is a live ball and considered to be "in play." Flags may not be removed for any reason.

Corner Kick - A direct kick from the corner area, taken by the attacking team when the defense last played the ball over the goal line.

Cross - A pass from one side of the playing field to the other, usually executed near the goal to help position the attacking team to score.

Direct Kick - A free kick that may be kicked directly into the opponent's goal.

Dribbling - Controlling the ball on the ground by using light taps with your feet.

Drop Ball - A ball dropped by the referee between players. A drop ball is used to restart the game after 1) an injury, 2) the ball hit a foreign object, or 3) the referee purposely stopped the game.

Forwards - Those players who generally shoot for goals. Forwards are composed of wings along the touchlines and strikers on the inside.

Free Kick - An unchallenged kick following a violation by the opponent.

Fullbacks - The players who form the defense right in front of the goalkeeper.

Goal Area - The area immediately in front of the goal, measuring 20 yards long, 6 yards wide.

Goalkeeper - The only player who may use his/her hands to play the ball. Primary duties are to defend the goal cage and keep the opponent from scoring.

Goal Kick - A kick from the goal area, taken by the defending team when the attacking team last played the ball over the goal line.

Halfbacks - Positioned in the middle of the team formation, these players are the links between the fullbacks and the forwards.

Half-Volley - A kick made on the short hop. Goalkeepers sometimes drop-kick the ball. This type of kick is a half-volley.

Indirect Kick - A free kick that may not go directly into the goal. After it has been kicked, someone else on either team must touch the ball for the goal to score.

Kickabout - An informal game of soccer, for exercise, ball control, and passing.

Linespersons - Officials who work the length of the touchlines, one on each side. Their primary duties are to signal offside and out of bounds calls and to assist the referee with the general control of the game.

Marking - Staying very close to your opponent, positioning yourself so as to intercept the ball when it is passed. A form of man-to-man defense. Be careful, however, that you do not commit an "obstruction" (see below).

Obstruction - The act of deliberately placing yourself in the path of an opponent, but making no attempt to play the ball.

Offside - A player is offside if, while in the opponent's half of the field and intending to receive the ball, he/she is beyond all defenders other than the goalkeeper. The offside is determined at the moment the ball is played. The penalty for being offside is an indirect free kick for the opponent. It is ultimately left to the referee whether to call an offside and award the free kick. If the referee feels that the attacking team will not benefit from the offside field position, he/she may refuse to call the offside and allow play to continue.

Outsides - The two forwards positioned closest to the touchlines, one on each side of the forward formation. Also known as wings, these players work the ball to the inside forwards or strikers for scoring.

Penalty Arc - The arc at the top of the penalty area. No player may be in this area when a penalty kick is being taken.

Penalty Area - The large area in front of the goal. It measures 18 x 44 yards. All direct fouls committed by the defense in this area result in penalty kicks. The goalkeeper may touch the ball anywhere in this area unless it was deliberately kicked to him/her by a teammate.

Penalty Kick - A penalty kick is taken 12 yards from the goal. It is given when a direct foul occurs in the penalty area (see above).

Referee - The official ultimately in charge of the entire game, including the time before kickoff, during halftime, and after the game is over.

Strikers - The two inside forwards whose primary task is to score goals. Strikers may gain possession of the ball by taking it directly from an opponent, or by receiving it from a teammate, usually a wing or a halfback.

Sweeper - A roving player who backs up the defense. (Equivalent of a football free safety.)

Tackling - Using the feet to take the ball away from an opponent. May be done standing or sliding, but tackler must avoid kicking or tripping the opponent.

Throw-in - When the ball goes out of bounds by crossing over the touchlines, the opponent of the team which last touched the ball puts it back in play with a throw-in, executed at the spot on the touchline where the ball went out of bounds. The thrower may stand on, but not over, the touchline. The ball must be thrown with both hands held over the head. Some part of both feet must be on the ground when the ball is released. A goal may not be scored directly from a throw-in, and the thrower may not play the ball again until another player has done so.

Touchlines - The boundary lines along the sides of the playing field. The boundary lines along the ends of the playing field are called goal lines.

Trapping - Getting the ball under control by using any part of your body other than your hands. Only the goalkeeper may play the ball with his/her hands, and only in the penalty area.

Wall - A defensive tactic in which at least three defenders line up shoulder-to-shoulder to defend against a free kick near their goal. The "human wall" must be at least 10 yards from the ball, or on the goal line between the goal posts.

THE YOUNG PLAYERS OF TODAY WILL BE OUR STARS OF TOMORROW!

Please help support U.S. Soccer's National Teams Programs.

YES! I want to support U.S. Soccer's National Teams Programs.
Enclosed is my donation of:

Gold Medal Level   ___ $500

Silver Medal Level   ___ $250

Bronze Medal Level   ___ $100

                                 ___ $50

                                   ___ $25

                                   ___   Other $____

Please make checks payable to:

U.S. Soccer Federation, Inc
c/o U.S. Soccer
Soccer House
1801-1811 S. Prairie Avenue
Chicago, IL 60616

*All donations will be used to support our
U.S. National Soccer Teams Programs and are tax deductible.*

Thank you for your support.